UGLY BETTY

LEVEL 2

SCHOLASTIC

Adapted by: Jane Rollason

Publisher: Jacquie Bloese

Commissioning Editor: Helen Parker

Editor: Cheryl Pelteret

Designer: Dawn Wilson

Picture research: Pupak Navabpour

Photo credits: Unless otherwise credited below, all photography © 2007 American Broadcasting Companies, Inc.
Pages 4 & 5: A Schein/Corbis; F Roberts/Alamy.
Pages 10, 38, 41, 46, 47, 48 & 49: Nicholas Cope.
Page 30: Courtesy of the Ugly Betty art department.
Pages 42 & 43: C Newsmakers/Getty/Newscom; C Steer/Stockphoto.
Page 52: H Shiffman/Stockphoto; M Lee, D Hurst/Alamy.

Ugly Betty © 2007 ABC Studios. All Rights Reserved
Text and cover art copyright © 2007 ABC Studios.
All Rights Reserved.

Published by Scholastic Ltd. 2009

No part of this publication may be reproduced in whole or in part, or stored in a retrieval system, or transmitted in any form or by any means, electronic, mechanical, photocopying, recording or otherwise, without written permission of the publisher. For information regarding permission write to:

Mary Glasgow Magazines (Scholastic Ltd.)
Euston House
24 Eversholt Street
London NW1 IDB

All rights reserved

Printed in Singapore. This edition printed in 2010.

Contents

	Page
Ugly Betty: Series 1	
People and Places	**4–5**
Episode guide	**6–41**
Making Ugly Betty	**42–43**
Interviews with the stars	**44–45**
Interiors: How to get the Suarez look	**46–47**
Interiors: How to get the *Mode* look	**48–49**
Fashion: Cool or uncool? by Justin Suarez	**50–51**
Advice from Betty, Marc and Amanda	**52–53**
Self-study activities	**54–56**
New Words	**inside back cover**

PEOPLE AND PLACES

QUEENS, NEW YORK CITY

Queens is in New York City, but it's very different from Manhattan. Lots of Latin American families, like the Suarez family, live here. Everybody knows everybody else here.

BETTY SUAREZ has always lived in Queens. She gets her first job at *Mode* magazine, as assistant to the editor. She has a boyfriend called Walter. He's from Queens too.

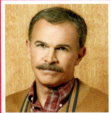

IGNACIO SUAREZ is Betty's dad. He's Mexican and he came to the USA thirty years ago. His wife Rosa died many years ago.

HILDA SUAREZ is Betty's older sister. She has a son called **JUSTIN**. Her job is selling slimming pills.

MANHATTAN, NEW YORK CITY

The *Mode* magazine office is in Manhattan in New York City. Fashion people live and work around here. They make fun of anyone who isn't cool.

BRADFORD MEADE is very rich. His business, Meade Publications, owns lots of magazines.

DANIEL MEADE is the new editor of *Mode* magazine. He's Bradford's son and he doesn't know much about magazines.

WILHELMINA SLATER is *Mode's* creative director. She wanted the editor's job. She still wants it, and she will do anything to get it. She's dangerous.

CLAIRE MEADE is Daniel's mother. Life has been very difficult for her since her older son, **ALEX MEADE**, died. He died in a sports accident.

MARC is Wilhelmina's assistant. He is best friends with Amanda.

HENRY GRUBSTICK works in Accounts at *Mode*. He knows lots of facts, like how many stars are in the sky. Betty likes him and he likes her too.

AMANDA is *Mode's* receptionist. Marc and Amanda can't believe Betty is working at *Mode*. It's a fashion magazine, but she doesn't know anything about fashion!

UGLY BETTY
SERIES 1 EPISODE GUIDE

EPISODE 1
'I'm the ugly girl. Your dad gave me a job? Remember?'

Betty Suarez has just finished college*. She is very surprised when she gets a job at a top fashion magazine, *Mode*. She doesn't know much about fashion!

Daniel Meade is starting a new job too. He's the editor of *Mode* magazine. His father, Bradford Meade, owns *Mode* magazine. But Daniel has a problem with women – he has a different girlfriend every day of the week. So Bradford offers Betty the job of Daniel's assistant. Why? Maybe then Daniel will think about his job more.

Not everyone at *Mode* is happy about the new editor. Wilhelmina Slater, the creative director, wants the job herself. She has a plan. She wants Daniel's first magazine to be terrible.

* college: in British English, we say university.

Daniel has to do a big story for Fabia Make-Up for his first magazine. And he doesn't ask for Wilhelmina's help. That's his first mistake.

He chooses a photographer. The photographer is a good friend of Wilhelmina's. That's Daniel's second mistake.

The photographer suggests pictures of models in front of crashed cars. Daniel thinks this is a cool idea.

Betty arrives at *Mode* the next day in very uncool clothes. She is very excited but Daniel wants a beautiful assistant. He gives Betty terrible things to do and hopes that she will leave. Betty wants to tell Daniel her idea for the Fabia story, but Daniel doesn't want to listen.

Finally, Daniel asks Betty to take part in the Fabia photos with tall, beautiful models. Everyone laughs at Betty and she walks out of the job. Daniel then understands that Betty is a real person with a real heart.

Daniel shows his photographs for the Fabia story to Fabia herself. She is very important to *Mode* magazine. In the photos, the models are in front of a car crash. But Daniel doesn't know that Fabia had a bad car crash a month before. Wilhelmina knows. Fabia is very angry and walks out.

Bradford is ready to fire Daniel. He gives Daniel 24 hours to think of a new story. That night Daniel sees Betty's idea on his desk. He loves it and he asks her to come back to *Mode*.

The next day they show Betty's idea to Fabia. It's about happy times between mothers and daughters. Fabia loves it. Daniel keeps his job. Daniel and Betty become friends.

Wilhelmina visits a strange woman in hospital. They discuss the future of Mode *magazine. Who is this woman?*

EPISODE 2

'These people aren't going to change. You have to change.'

Daniel's brother Alex was a magazine editor too. But then Alex died in an accident.

Daniel wants to make some changes to *Mode*. He and Betty look at new ideas. Betty likes the photographer, Vincent Bianchi.

'Bianchi will never work here,' Daniel says, 'because he hated my brother Alex.'

Betty discovers that Bianchi is from Queens. She phones him and asks him to meet Daniel for lunch. Bianchi agrees because he and Betty went to the same school. Bianchi wants Betty to come to the lunch too.

Hilda gives Betty a Queens makeover, with big hair and scary make-up. Wilhelmina makes fun of Betty in front of everyone.

Betty knows she doesn't look right. She doesn't want to join Daniel and Bianchi for lunch now. So Amanda goes to the restaurant and tells Bianchi that she is Betty. Bianchi guesses right away. Daniel says he's sorry. Bianchi likes Daniel and he agrees to do the photos for the magazine.

Wilhelmina is very angry, because things are going well for Daniel.

The woman in hospital calls Daniel. She gives him a strange message about his father Bradford. What's going on?

EPISODE 3

'If you control The Book, you control the magazine.'

Daniel's second *Mode* magazine has a story about film star Natalie Whitman. Natalie looks a bit fatter than usual in the photos, but she and Betty like the photos.

Daniel and Wilhelmina only want very thin people in *Mode*. So they fake her photos.

Daniel learns about The Book. The Book is the page-by-page plan for the next magazine. It's top secret! He's the editor, so he should take The Book home every night. Except ... where is it? Wilhelmina has it. Daniel says he will take The Book from now on.

Wilhelmina takes the faked photos of Natalie out of The Book and puts in the real photos. She wants to make trouble for Daniel (again).

Natalie joins Betty for lunch in the *Mode* dining room.

'You look great as you are,' Betty tells Natalie. 'I love those photos of the real you.'

'You say what you really think,' says Natalie. 'I like that.'

When Daniel leaves the office, he forgets The Book. So

Betty takes it home. In the morning, The Book isn't there. Gina lives next door to Betty, and she took it during the night. Gina is always fighting with Hilda. Now she wants $4,000 for The Book. Betty lies to Daniel and says she's bringing The Book back to the office. She doesn't tell him about Gina because she thinks she'll lose her job.

Someone tells Wilhelmina about Gina and she sends Marc to Queens with the money. He gets The Book from Gina.

When *Mode* appears, the 'wrong' photos are in it. Wilhelmina and Marc wait for the trouble to start. Daniel doesn't try to save himself. He says it was his fault, and Betty leaves *Mode*. But Natalie loves the photos! They show the real her.

Betty gets her job back and Bradford is pleased with Daniel.

EPISODE 4
'I believe fashion is good for you!'

Everyone's favourite room at the office is the *Mode* Clothes Cupboard. It's full of wonderful clothes and bags used in the photos. Every three months, Christina empties the cupboard. Free clothes for everyone. But you have to fight for them!

Marc wants the Gucci bag. It costs $4,500 new.

'Why don't you buy a fake?' Betty asks Marc.

'The fakes are nothing like the real thing,' he says.

Betty isn't interested in the free clothes. They are all for tall, thin girls. She's busy anyway. Daniel has asked her to send in his expenses. Betty asks Marc for help. That's a mistake. He gives her Wilhelmina's fake expenses. 'Copy these,' he says.

Henry works in the Accounts office. When he gets Daniel's (fake) expenses from Betty, he stops Daniel's *Mode* account. Daniel has to take someone important out to dinner. His name is Oshi, and he has his own fashion business. Daniel now has only $327. A bottle of Oshi's favourite champagne costs more than that! Daniel is worried. Oshi is very difficult to please. He only likes the colour white. Betty has an idea ... .

There are money problems at the Suarez house too. Ignacio has a heart problem. He needs to take pills but they are very expensive.

Christina has a surprise for Betty. It's the expensive Gucci bag from the clothes cupboard. Betty sells it and buys her dad's pills. Her boyfriend Walter finds out and buys her a fake Gucci bag.

Oshi arrives at *Mode*. Daniel has no money, so Wilhelmina says she will take him out. Daniel isn't happy about this, but what can he do? But then Betty runs in with news that Wilhelmina has put in fake expenses.

Daniel has to take Oshi out himself. Now what was Betty's idea? A burger bar. It's cheap. But it's unusual too, because it's white! What will Oshi say? A white burger bar? ... He loves it!

Betty sells the fake Gucci bag to Marc. He thinks it's real.

EPISODE 5

'By midday on Thursday, someone will lose their job.'

The next *Mode* magazine is going to be about the end of the world. The idea is top secret!

Everyone goes to a cool party for magazine people. 'Fat' Carol from *Mode* is going out with the editor of *Isabella*, another fashion magazine. She tells him all about the 'top secret' idea. Marc, Betty and Amanda all talk to *Isabella* people about the idea at the party too.

When the next *Isabella* magazine appears, guess what? It's about the end of the world. 'Someone will lose their job for this,' says Wilhelmina. Marc, Betty and Amanda all think it's their fault.

But then Wilhelmina finds out about 'Fat' Carol and the *Isabella* editor. So Marc, Betty and Amanda are safe.

Walter *was* Betty's boyfriend. But then he went out with Gina next door. Later, Walter learned that Gina only wanted him to get her a new TV. Now Walter wants Betty back.

> 'We must tell Daniel about Bradford and Fey,' says the woman in hospital to Wilhelmina. What does she mean?

EPISODE 6

'Two men are fighting over you? You're lucky.'

Betty gets an email from Amanda. 'Don't forget to wear Halloween clothes,' it says. So Betty comes to the office in Halloween clothes. But everyone else is wearing their usual cool clothes.

'What about the email?' says Betty to Amanda. And then Betty understands. 'Ah! You only sent it to me,' she says.

Amanda and Marc smile at each other. Amanda is very pleased with herself. But they can't upset Betty so easily.

'I guess I win, then,' she says. 'I'm wearing the best Halloween clothes!'

Daniel has a different girlfriend every day of the week. He's left his watch in one girl's apartment. Which one? He can't remember! Betty has to find it. Amanda was his girl on Monday, and she has it. She tells Betty that she's in love with Daniel.

Betty has love problems too. Is Walter the right man for her? She doesn't know. She really likes Henry from Accounts. Henry invites her to lunch. Walter sees them in the restaurant and she feels bad.

Betty learns a secret about her father: Ignacio came into the USA as an illegal immigrant* thirty years ago.

> *'I think it's time for Fey to come back,'* says the woman in hospital. What does she mean?

* An illegal immigrant comes into a country secretly, without the correct papers.

EPISODE 7

'Sofia thinks I only got the job because of my father.'

Daniel sees a beautiful woman in the lift and falls in love. He doesn't know who she is.

'She probably works at one of the other magazines,' he thinks.

Betty, Hilda and Ignacio go to see a lawyer. 'You've been in the USA for thirty years, Mr Suarez,' says the lawyer. 'Why haven't you got a green card*?' There's something he isn't telling them. The lawyer can help him, but he wants $20,000!

Hilda finds a cheaper lawyer. This lawyer only wants $5,000.

Daniel goes to a Meade editors' meeting. The woman from the lift is there by the coffee.

'Ah, she's a waitress,' he thinks.

'Mine's black with two sugars,' he says to her.

The meeting starts. 'We have a new Meade magazine,' says Bradford. 'It's called *Modern Young Woman (MYW)*, and here is the new editor, Sofia Reyes.'

It's the woman from the lift! Daniel feels really stupid.

* Immigrants to the US must get a green card if they want to work.

Hilda comes to *Mode* to sell her slimming pills. The Suarez family need the money for the new lawyer. Wilhelmina sends Hilda away.

Ignacio tells his daughters about their mother. 'When I met your mother she was already married,' he says. 'I was their cook. But her husband – he was a terrible man. He hit her all the time. One day, I tried to stop him and he pulled out a knife. I hit him many times … and then … I killed him. We ran away. We came to the USA, but I never tried to get a green card.'

> *Wilhelmina and the woman in the hospital are planning to take control of the business. Who is she? And what about Daniel?*

EPISODE 8
'Don't be afraid,' Betty tells herself. 'It's just a hotel.'

Every time Daniel and Sofia have a conversation, it's a fight. Daniel never wins. He's really in love with Sofia.

Sofia asks Betty to help her with a story for *MYW*.

Daniel has never asked Betty to write for *Mode*. But he wants to please Sofia. So he asks Betty to write about a hotel for *Mode*.

Walter has planned a weekend in Atlantic City with Betty.

'I'm sorry, Walter,' says Betty. 'But I really want to write this story for *Mode*.'

She loves the hotel. She never goes to places like this. Walter joins her and they go to the hotel restaurant. The people in the hotel don't like people from Queens.

'This isn't the right place for us,' Walter says to Betty, and walks out.

Betty tries to write her story like a *Mode* writer. But Walter's right. She can't do it. She writes the story in her own 'Betty' style.

Hilda asks Justin's father, Santos, for the money for the lawyer. Santos says she can have the money – but he wants to see his son. She feels sorry for Santos and invites him to their Thanksgiving* dinner.

Daniel and Sofia go on a date and have a great time. Daniel thinks they are now going out together.

Daniel thinks Betty's hotel story is great, but it's not right for *Mode*. Sofia finds Betty in the toilets. She's crying about her story. Sofia loves her story and prints it in *MYW*.

Daniel comes to look for Sofia.

'I've been thinking about you all weekend,' Daniel says to Sofia.

'I'm sorry,' Sofia says, 'I was busy ... with my boyfriend.'

---

* Thanksgiving Day is the fourth Thursday in November. Americans have a holiday and a big family meal.

EPISODE 9

'I'm so busy with my job – I'm never at home.'

Hilda's cheap lawyer only wants $5,000. But Gina from next door knows about this lawyer and tells Betty.

'Be careful, Betty,' says Gina. 'I know a woman in the next street. She needed a lawyer to get her children back. This lawyer took her money but she didn't help her.'

Betty tells Hilda, but Hilda won't listen.

'You're feeling bad,' says Hilda, 'because *I'm* looking after the family. You're too busy with your job.'

'I don't want to go to my parents' Thanksgiving party,' Daniel tells Betty. 'It's always so boring.' But then he learns that Bradford has invited Sofia and her boyfriend.

Betty is cooking their Thanksgiving meal with her dad when Daniel phones. She runs across town to his flat.

'What do you think?' he asks when she gets there. 'What shall I wear to my parents' Thanksgiving party? The purple shirt or the white one? I want to look good for Sofia.'

Betty can't believe it. He phoned her to ask her that?! 'This is *my* family holiday,' she says. 'The purple one.'

Santos arrives with a big present for Justin. The lawyer comes and Hilda gives her the money. She invites the lawyer to Thanksgiving dinner that evening.

Daniel meets Sofia's boyfriend at his parents' party. He is blond, handsome and funny. His name is Hunter and he helps the poor and dances beautifully. Sofia tells Daniel she wants to marry Hunter.

Bradford suddenly sees a woman at the party. She looks like Fey Summers.

Fey was the editor of Mode *before Daniel. Bradford and Fey were lovers for twenty years ... and then she died in a car crash.*

'I saw Fey just now,' he says to Claire, his wife. 'She's alive.'

'What are you talking about?' says Claire. 'She's dead! She died in a car crash. Remember?'

The Suarez family waits for the lawyer to come to dinner, but she doesn't come. The dinner is cold. Hilda is sorry that she didn't listen to Betty.

'It's my fault,' says Betty. 'I'm so busy with my job, I'm never here.'

'You took care of us when Mum died,' says Hilda. 'You can't live through your family. You've got to have your own life.'

Betty gets a call from Daniel. 'I won't answer it,' she says.

'Go on,' says Hilda. 'Answer it. Say hi to Daniel for me.' Daniel's been in a bar all evening. He's unhappy about Sofia and her boyfriend. Betty takes him home to Queens.

EPISODE 10
'Today, Betty, you are the boss!'

Daniel feels ill so he stays in bed at the Suarez house. Betty goes into the office.

Sofia is there. She wants to talk to Daniel. She's not sure about Hunter.

Hilda tells Justin that a Christmas tree is too expensive this year. Daniel orders one for them.

Everyone is excited at *Mode*. Some famous rock stars are bringing their new baby into the office. The baby is called Baby Chutney, and only *Mode* will have photos of her in their next magazine. But they only have three hours to take the photos.

Wilhelmina and Marc take a taxi to the airport to collect Baby Chutney. But Wilhelmina upsets the taxi driver and he leaves them in a poor part of town.

Daniel loves the family feeling in the Suarez house. The Christmas tree looks nice. Betty calls Daniel from the office. 'Where are you?' she cries.

'Today, Betty,' he says, '*you* are the boss.'

The photographer arrives. He's too cool to talk to Betty. He says the baby is really ugly.

'Babies are never ugly,' says Betty. She fires the photographer. Then Daniel calls. 'Let's do the photos here at your house, in front of the Christmas tree. It's like a real Christmas in an ordinary family home.'

Everyone goes to Queens. On the way, Sofia offers Betty a job on *MYW*.

Sofia says Hunter is not right for her. She wants to be with Daniel. Sofia tells Daniel about the job offer.

'I don't want to leave my job,' Betty says to Daniel.

'But you can't say no to this job with Sofia,' says Daniel.

EPISODE 11
'I guess this is goodbye.'

'We have to save money,' says Daniel at the next *Mode* editorial meeting.

'How about having the Christmas party in the office?' says Betty.

Betty is leaving to work at *MYW*, so Amanda is going to be Daniel's new assistant.

Betty goes to Walter's Christmas party. It's horrible! Betty doesn't think she loves Walter.

Betty talks to Henry from Accounts at the *Mode* Christmas party. They get on very well. In fact, they're starting to fall in love. But later Henry kisses a supermodel. Betty sees him and runs home.

Henry calls Betty. He wants to tell her that he didn't kiss the model; *she* kissed *him*! Hilda speaks to him on the phone. But she doesn't tell Betty he called. She thinks Walter is the right guy for Betty, not Henry.

> *Bradford finds out for sure that Fey is dead. He knows that someone is trying to trick him. The woman at his party wasn't Fey. But who sent her?*

EPISODE 12
'I think I fit in better at Mode than MYW.'

Betty starts her new job at *MYW*. The first girl she meets is just like her.

Sofia wants Betty to write a story about her time at *Mode*. Sofia tells Betty that she's losing Daniel. She starts crying. Hunter has gone to Europe.

Betty goes up to the *Mode* office and tells Daniel. (That's just what Sofia wanted.)

'What do I have to do?' asks Daniel.

'Ask her to marry you,' says Betty.

Betty is in the street. She sees Sofia and Hunter. They don't see Betty. Sofia gives Hunter some money. He's a dancer in a nightclub! Betty and Christina go to the club.

Betty calls to tell Daniel about Hunter.

'Betty,' says Daniel. 'I've just asked Sofia to marry me. She said yes!' He sounds very happy so Betty doesn't tell him about Hunter.

The next day at *MYW*, Betty asks Sofia about Hunter.

'I used Hunter. I wanted to find out how much Daniel loved me,' says Sofia. 'Now I'm going to the TV station. We are going on Breakfast TV to tell the world about our wedding.'

'I'll come,' says Betty.

'You stay here, Betty,' says Sofia. 'Write that story about *Mode* for me.'

Betty finds The Book for *MYW*. The main story is about Daniel and Sofia's wedding. Betty can't believe it. Sofia never loved Daniel; she only wanted a big story for her first magazine.

Daniel doesn't know anything about this. He's going to look stupid on TV, when he finds out that Sofia has tricked him. Betty runs to the TV station to tell Daniel, but she can't get in.

Sofia makes fun of Daniel on TV. Daniel leaves the TV building and disappears.

The woman in hospital calls Wilhelmina. 'Our plan hasn't worked,' she says. 'Bradford knows that Fey is really dead. Now we need proof that he killed her.'

EPISODE 13

'Betty, he looks at you in a special way. I know that look.'

Hilda loses her job. Some people using the slimming pills lost all their hair. Betty has left *MYW*. She's working in a Mexican restaurant.

Wilhelmina is deciding who is 'In' or 'Out' at *Mode*. She's planning to take control of *Mode* very soon. Marc helps her. Wilhelmina decides that Amanda's 'Out'.

Daniel is in Rio. Betty goes to his flat to welcome him home. He's not in Rio. He's been in his flat all the time. He never went to Rio. Sofia has broken his heart and the world is laughing at him. He's on every front page of every New York newspaper.

'When I go back to *Mode*, will you come back with me?' Daniel asks. Betty is very happy. So now Daniel has two assistants – Betty and Amanda. Amanda isn't pleased.

Betty gets a date for Daniel with supermodel Gisele. But Amanda wants to make trouble for Betty. She secretly calls Gisele and tells her that the date is off. Daniel arrives at the restaurant. Photographers are outside the window. He's going to look stupid again. Gisele doesn't appear. He calls Betty. Betty turns up with some work so it looks like a business dinner.

Daniel and Betty escape from the photographers and take a walk across Brooklyn Bridge. 'Henry really likes you, Betty,' he tells her. 'I've seen the way he looks at you. I know that look.'

'He kissed a supermodel at the Christmas party,' says Betty.

'Hey,' says Daniel. 'That supermodel kissed every man in the room. I was there, remember?'

Daniel tells Betty about his brother.

'You never talk about him,' says Betty.

'I still can't believe he's dead,' says Daniel.

Marc tells Amanda that Wilhelmina will soon be the new editor of *Mode*. Amanda moves to Wilhelmina's team. She knows that a big change is coming at *Mode*. She doesn't want to be on Daniel's side so she goes back to her job as *Mode's* receptionist. Betty gets her desk back.

'I have proof,' says Wilhelmina. 'We can put Bradford Meade in prison.' Wilhelmina gives Christina a letter to take to the local police station. The 'proof' is in the letter.
The woman in hospital gets ready to leave. Who is she?

EPISODE 14

'Here at Mode I'm Betty. Everywhere else I'm Hilda's sister.'

Bradford is pleased with Daniel. He's doing well with *Mode*. Bradford's planning to give control of Meade Publications to him.

Hilda arrives at the *Mode* office. It's Fashion Week and *Mode* needs lots of help. Hilda wants a job. Betty learns that Henry left a phone message after the Christmas party. Daniel offers Hilda a job. Betty is not happy – *Mode* is her life, not Hilda's.

Mode's party is called 'Ten new faces to watch'. One of the ten is Christina, from the Clothes Cupboard. How did she get a place in the ten? Remember that letter she took to the police station? She didn't want to help Wilhelmina. But she doesn't want to work in the Clothes Cupboard for the rest of her life.

Everyone loves Hilda at Fashion Week. She does the make-up and hair for the models. They invite her to parties. Betty is very upset. All their lives, Betty has been 'Hilda's sister'. She doesn't want Hilda to take control at *Mode*. So she fires her.

There's a very beautiful supermodel at the *Mode* party. Nobody knows her. Daniel talks to her. She asks him about his brother. 'In some ways, life is easier for me now, because he's dead,' says Daniel.

Hilda and Betty become friends again.

> *Alex Meade didn't die in an accident. The woman in the hospital is Alex, but now Alex has become Alexis.*

***

Alexis wears one of Christina's designs. Bradford comes to the microphone and starts to speak at the *Mode* party. Alexis pushes him to one side.

'Bradford hasn't lost a son,' she tells the party. 'He's got a daughter.'

'Oooh!' says everyone.

'Hi, Daddy,' says Alexis. 'I'm back.'

The police arrive. They say that Bradford killed Fey Summers and they take him away.

EPISODE 15

'Find someone who loves you,' said Betty's mum before she died.

Daniel visits his dad in prison. There is a lot of proof against Bradford – emails, phone calls, Fey's car. Did his father kill her? Daniel doesn't know what to think.

Henry invites Betty to a show. Betty says Walter's still around. 'Let's go just as friends,' says Betty.

'Great!' says Henry.

Daniel has an editorial meeting. Alexis comes in. She's got some lawyer's papers. 'The papers say, if Bradford Meade cannot control the business, his son Alexander Meade will take control. That's me! I'm in control now. The new editor of *Mode* is Wilhelmina Slater. And, Daniel, you're fired.'

Daniel's lawyer stops Alexis. Wilhelmina can't be editor yet. She has to wait. She walks out.

Walter gets a better job. That's good, but it's in another city. Betty must decide – is her future with him or not?

Claire Meade arrives at *Mode* with new dresses for Alexis. She wants to take her children out to dinner. Daniel doesn't want her in the office.

'I'm worried about my mother,' Daniel tells Betty. 'I have to watch her. I'll take her home.'

Just then Walter arrives. Betty doesn't want to talk to him. She offers to take Claire home.

Betty tells Claire about Walter. 'My mum once said, "The most important thing in life is to find someone who loves you." Well, Walter loves me.'

'You're not happy right now,' says Claire. 'And mothers only want their children to be happy.'

When Betty gets back to *Mode*, she stops a fight between Daniel and Alexis. She takes them to Coney Island*, where Claire is waiting.

'Dad knows that I wanted to be a woman,' says Alexis. 'Now he never wants to see me again.'

'Why didn't you tell me?' asks Daniel.

---

* Coney Island is New York's fair.

'Because you're just like Dad,' says Alexis.

Daniel doesn't think he is like Bradford. He is very upset.

***

Walter is waiting for Betty outside her house. Walter already knows that she doesn't love him. They kiss and say goodbye.

In the office the next day, Henry comes to see Betty. Betty is very excited about the show, until he gives her both tickets.

'Listen, Betty,' he says. 'I went to my parents' place at Christmas. I met up with my old girlfriend. I was unhappy after the party here. So we started to see each other. And, well, yesterday, she arrived here. You're with Walter. Why don't you take Walter to the show?'

Betty doesn't tell him that she has finished with Walter.

Daniel and Alexis agree to work together. Wilhelmina is very angry.

Betty goes to help Claire. Her house is empty and she's unhappy.

'Don't worry,' says Betty, 'your husband will be home soon.'

'Maybe,' says Claire. 'Maybe not.'

'He's not a killer,' says Betty.

'I know. And I know who killed Fey Summers. It wasn't Bradford. *It was me.*'

EPISODE 16
'Fight for your little dream.'

Bradford tells Daniel to get him a good lawyer.
Betty tells Daniel that his mother killed Fey.

Later, Betty meets a nice girl in the dining room. Her name's Charlie and she's new in New York. They get on well. Daniel has given Betty tickets to a fashion party. Betty invites her new friend to go with her. Then she learns that Charlie is Henry's girlfriend.

Alexis finds out that her old friends are not real friends. Her phone never rings. So Wilhelmina takes her out for the evening. In a bar, some men make fun of Alexis. They know that she was a man before. Wilhelmina hits one of the men very hard.

On the way to the party, Betty loses Charlie. Betty knows Charlie will be frightened, alone in New York. She calls Henry and they try to find Charlie. Betty tells Henry about Walter. They find Charlie a few hours later. She loves New York! She's decided to stay! Betty gives Henry the tickets for the party.

Wilhelmina comes back to *Mode*. She is angry with Alexis, but she is still the creative director of *Mode*. She wants the magazine to look good because it will have her name on it.

EPISODE 17
'Henry, we're just two people who work in the same building.'

Alexis hates Bradford. She wants him to stay in prison.

Bradford wants a top lawyer. He asks Daniel to get Grace Chin for him – she's the best. Bradford doesn't know that Daniel was at college with Grace. And that's not all! He asked her out on a date, but then he found a prettier girl. Grace waited three hours for Daniel in the snow.

Daniel calls her. She meets him. She is still very angry

with him. But she still likes Daniel. She thinks she can get Bradford out of prison. Daniel doesn't tell Alexis about Grace.

Grace wants to speak to Claire, but Daniel won't let his mother speak to the lawyer. 'Mum will tell Grace that she killed Fey,' Daniel thinks.

Henry and Charlie invite Betty to Charlie's birthday party.

'Why are you going?' Christina asks Betty. 'At least take a date with you.' Betty decides to ask her dentist.

Alexis finds out that that Grace Chin is working for Bradford. Alexis is angry because Grace is the best lawyer in New York City. Alexis is afraid she'll get Bradford out of prison. Alexis doesn't know that Daniel found Grace. She also doesn't know that Daniel is spending a lot of time with Grace.

Alexis and Daniel are getting on well, so Wilhelmina decides to make trouble. She sends Marc to follow Daniel and take photos of Daniel with Grace. It doesn't take long.

Wilhelmina takes the proof to Alexis. She can't believe it. 'Daniel lied to me. He said that he didn't know Grace Chin.'

Grace finds out that Claire killed Fey.

'You left me in the snow for three hours,' Grace tells Daniel. 'Now I'm leaving you. How do you like it?'

Claire wants to disappear. She calls Betty because she needs some money. Betty has a *Mode* card – perhaps Betty can give her some money. She stops at the Suarez house on her way to the airport.

'Don't run, Mrs Meade,' says Betty. 'Stay and tell the police what happened.' Claire calls the police and tells them that she killed Fey.

EPISODE 18
'How about a letter from the heart?'

Betty feels bad. Claire is in prison because of her.

Bradford and Alexis meet. 'You and I – we're finished,' says Bradford.

Bradford tries to fire Alexis, but then remembers that Claire owns *Mode*. She won't agree. She wants Alexis and Daniel to be editors together.

Wilhelmina has a new plan. Alexis and Daniel must hate each other. Then while they are fighting, she can take control. She tells Alexis to put herself on the front of *Mode*. Alexis agrees because it will upset Bradford.

Daniel asks Alexis to write a *Letter from the Editor*. Daniel plans to write one too, and the letters will be next to each other. Except that ... he doesn't write his *Letter from the editor*. One of the *Mode* writers writes it for him. Betty can't believe it. He's lying to his readers.

Daniel's *Letter to the Editor* is about shoes.

'Your mother's in prison, your brother's become your sister, and you're writing about shoes?' says Betty. 'How about a letter from the heart?'

Daniel writes his new letter and shows Betty. Betty discovers that Alexis has already taken The Book. It's too late. Daniel can't stop Alexis. The magazine will appear – with Daniel's fake letter about shoes.

'I can't go on,' says Daniel. 'Alex always got there first. Now Alexis will always get there first. There are lots of parties out there in the city. That's what I'm good at – going to parties.'

With Daniel out of the way, Alexis decides to stay as editor. Wilhelmina thinks of a new plan. She will marry Bradford, and become a Meade. Then she will have control of Meade Publications.

....

EPISODE 19
'Daniel hasn't changed his socks since Tuesday.'

Alexis is taking control. Daniel's going out every night. When he comes into the office, he looks terrible. Betty tries to help him, but he pushes her away.

'Daniel needs me right now,' Betty says to Christina. 'He hasn't changed his socks since Tuesday.'

'You need to have some fun, Betty,' says Christina.

'You're worrying about Daniel because you're upset about Henry.'

Daniel comes into the club with a group of friends. He doesn't know Betty is there. Betty sees a photographer trying to get a picture of him with a girl. She shouts his name. Daniel is very angry.

'Are you following me, Betty? Leave me alone. When we leave that building, your day is over.'

Betty leaves the club. She is upset by Daniel's words. Then Christina makes it worse. She tells Betty that she helped Wilhelmina. She gave her information about Daniel and took the papers about Bradford to the police station.

'Why did you agree to help Wilhelmina?' asks Betty.

'I don't want to be in the Clothes Cupboard all my life,' says Christina.

'*Mode* is the wrong place to look for friends,' says Betty, and goes home.

Daniel phones Betty later. Ignacio answers. Betty won't speak to Daniel. That's never happened before.

EPISODE 20

'When you gave me a job, you got more than an assistant.'

Betty stays in bed. She calls the office and says she's ill. She's still angry with Christina and Daniel and Henry. Hilda is doing a hairdressing course. Betty goes with her.

'A job is not about making friends, it's about making money,' says Hilda. And Hilda tells Betty, 'Sometimes, with friends, you have to forget the bad things.'

Wilhelmina wants Bradford to fall in love with her. Bradford wants Alexis to go. He hates the idea that his son is now a daughter. He doesn't want to see Alexis again. He offers Alexis ten million dollars.

'I'm not going anywhere,' says Alexis. 'You must pay for everything you've done to me. '

The editor of Brazil *Mode* is at the New York office. He's taking some photos for the magazine. His name is Rodrigo and he asks Alexis out. He knows she was once a man. They get on very well. Rodrigo invites Alexis to Brazil.

Hilda has started going out with Santos again. Ignacio isn't happy. 'It'll be just like last time,' he says. But it isn't. Santos has changed. He asks Hilda to marry him. What does Justin think?

'Don't marry him for me,' he says. 'Do it because you love him.'

Hilda says no to Santos. She thinks he will break her heart again.

'Now you're breaking *my* heart,' says Santos. So Hilda says yes.

Betty and Christina talk. Betty says she's sorry, and they're friends again.

Bradford and Wilhelmina talk about Rodrigo.

'Alexis and Rodrigo – that was a brilliant idea of yours,' says Bradford to Wilhelmina. 'You're the best!'

Ignacio gets bad news – they're sending him back to Mexico.

EPISODE 21
'Back off, Betty,' says Charlie. 'He's my boyfriend.'

Ignacio has to go back to Mexico and wait for a visa*. Then he can come back to the USA with the correct papers. Betty and Hilda can't find a cheap plane ticket.

At *Mode* it's Office Assistants' Day. Betty chooses a place in Times Square** for the party.

'They've got one of those horses,' she tells Christina. 'You know, if you stay on for 15 seconds, you win $1,000. That'll buy my dad's plane ticket!'

Daniel arrives at the office. Once again, he looks terrible. He gives Betty a cheap present for Office Assistants' Day.

Wilhelmina tries to make Bradford feel young again. She wants him to leave Claire and marry her.

Henry invites himself to Office Assistants' Day.

Betty gets on the horse. A man throws something at her

* A visa allows you to go into a country. It usually says how long you can stay.

** Times Square is a place for tourists. *Mode* people come here for a joke.

and she falls off after 14 seconds. Henry fights the guy who threw something. But Henry doesn't fight very well, and soon he's on the floor. Henry's girlfriend, Charlie, arrives and takes him home.

Alexis visits Claire in prison. 'I'm falling in love with Rodrigo,' she says. Claire tells her to follow her heart.

Claire gets another visitor. This time it's Wilhelmina. She wants Claire to leave Bradford. He's unhappy, she says.

'Of course he's unhappy,' says Claire. 'His wife is in prison. Now stay away from my husband.'

Wilhelmina's plan is not working. But then she has another idea.

'I'll tell Bradford that Claire sent two men to my house ... they came in and hit me,' Wilhelmina says to Marc. 'Claire has lots of friends in prison now – she could easily find people to do a thing like that.'

'So she knows you're going out with Bradford. She killed Fey – now she wants to kill you?' says Marc.

'That's right. Then Bradford will leave her and ... he'll marry me! Come on. Marc, hit me! Hit me hard! It must look bad.'

Alexis tells Rodrigo that she will come to Brazil with him. But then she hears him on the phone to Bradford.

'Take her to Brazil,' says Bradford. 'Keep her there.'

'I'll be editor of Brazil *Mode*, right?' says Rodrigo.

Alexis understands the trick. She hits Rodrigo and leaves. Back in her office, she rings a number.

'Kill Bradford Meade,' she says, 'and do it quickly.'

Bradford goes to see Wilhelmina. There was an accident: Marc pushed her downstairs by mistake. Now she looks terrible.

'Did Claire do this to you?' says Bradford to Wilhelmina.

'Then I'm leaving Claire.'

The next day, Daniel gives Betty a real present for Office Assistants' Day. Four plane tickets to Guadalajara!

....

EPISODE 22
'Fight for the man you love.'

Betty and her family travel to Mexico. Ignacio hasn't seen his family in Mexico for thirty years. On the plane, Betty draws the family tree. There are plenty of names on Ignacio's side. But her mother Rosa's side is empty.

'I don't know anything about Rosa's family,' says Ignacio crossly.

Hilda is thinking about her wedding to Santos. She hasn't found a wedding dress yet.

Betty learns from Ignacio's sister that Rosa's mother Yolanda is still living. Betty can't believe it.

'You didn't tell us that we have a grandmother?' she says to her father.

'She hated me because I was a cook,' says Ignacio. 'After Rosa married me, she never spoke to us again.'

Ignacio goes to get his visa. Betty takes Hilda on a bus out of the city. Yolanda lives in a little blue house in the middle of nowhere. But she is very old now and she thinks Betty is Rosa. 'You have always been in my heart,'

Yolanda tells Betty. 'Go with Ignacio. Fight for the man you love.'

She goes to her cupboard and gives Betty some of Rosa's clothes. One of them is Rosa's wedding dress. Hilda thinks it's beautiful.

Ignacio arrives in the village to collect Betty and Hilda. Before they leave, Ignacio speaks to the bar owner. As soon as Ignacio leaves, the bar owner takes out his phone and speaks to someone on it.

'Guess who just walked into town,' he says, 'Ignacio Suarez.'

Ignacio doesn't get his visa and he has to stay in Mexico.

EPISODE 23
'For one day, I was happy.'

Wilhelmina's plan has finally worked. Bradford asks her to marry him.

Betty and Henry meet in the office. Betty tells Henry

that she's going to fight for him. Henry says that he has finished with Charlie.

'She's not the one for me,' he says. Betty and Henry make their first date. Betty invites Henry to Queens for supper. Then they're planning to go out together.

Wilhemina and Hilda are both planning their weddings. Wilhelmina's will be a little more expensive than Hilda's.

Betty is cooking for Henry. Someone's at the front door.

'You're early,' calls Betty. She's very excited. But it's not Henry. It's Charlie, with some bad news.

'I'm going to have a baby,' Charlie says. 'Henry's baby.'

Then Henry arrives. He and Betty look at each other. This changes everything. They can never be together now.

The next day Betty and Henry meet for the last time in Central Park.

'For one day, I was happy,' says Betty to Henry.

Henry says he can't leave his child. Betty understands.

Claire escapes from prison.

●

Betty learns that Charlie has been dating her dentist for two months. Maybe it's not Henry's baby!

●

Justin is singing the star part in the school musical. Hilda is watching. Santos is on his way.

●

Daniel is losing control of his life. He takes too many pills. He goes to Alexis's office to say goodbye. Alexis sees that Daniel is in great danger. He must go to hospital or he will die. She drives him to hospital in Bradford's car. But halfway there, something goes wrong with the car. Alexis can't stop the car and it crashes. There's blood everywhere. Alexis and Daniel are not moving.

•

Santos stops at a shop to buy some sweets for Justin. There's a gunman in the shop. He wants the shopkeeper's money. Santos sees him. He tries to get the gun. They fight ... and the gunman kills Santos.

•

Hilda is still watching Justin. She looks at the empty seat next to her.

'Why is Santos always late?' she thinks.

Betty arrives at the school. She takes Hilda outside. She tells her the terrible news. And that's the end of Series 1.

Ugly Betty Series 1 ends with lots of questions.

Will Betty and Henry ever go out together?
Will Bradford marry Wilhelmina?
Will the police find Claire?
Are Daniel and Alexis dead?
Will Ignacio get back from Mexico?
How will Hilda and Justin live without Santos?
Will you watch Series 2?

MAKING

The first Ugly Betty

A new TV programme started in Colombia in 1999. It was called 'Yo Soy Betty, La Fea', which means 'I am Ugly Betty' in Spanish.

This Betty works at a fashion house called Ecomoda – she is the new assistant to the new boss. On her first day at work, she orders coffee on the telephone. 'How will I know you?' asks the guy from the coffee shop. 'I am Betty – the ugly one,' she answers. How sad!

Everyone laughs at her because of her glasses, braces* and terrible hair. But they don't know that she went to university and speaks five languages. And she could run Ecomoda without any help.

More than ten different countries have made their own Ugly Betty story, from Mexico to Israel.

* Many teenagers have to wear braces on their teeth like Betty.

The American Betty

The most important thing was to find the right Betty.

Silvio Horta wrote the first episode. He and the show's director and producers wanted America Ferrera to play Betty from the beginning. 'There was no other person for Betty,' says Silvio. 'America was the one.'

Betty is a girl from Queens with glasses, braces and terrible hair. She doesn't sound like a big star. So why do we love her?

'Everybody feels they don't fit in at some time in their lives,' says Silvio Horta. 'If you're pretty or ugly or thin or fat or poor or rich, you can see yourself in this girl.' Betty tells the world, 'This is me. I am not going to change, and I'm OK with that.' She gives everybody hope.

Ugly Betty

New York in Ugly Betty

This is a New York story. New York City is a star in the TV show. We see two very different sides of the city: life in Queens and life in Manhattan.

The show takes us to lots of famous New York places. Betty and Daniel talk about things on the Brooklyn Bridge. Betty loses Henry's girlfriend Charlie on the New York Subway. Henry and Betty say goodbye in Central Park. The Meade Publications building is a famous New York building in real life: the New York Life Insurance Building on Madison Avenue.

Over in Queens, life happens out on the colourful streets.

Wilhelmina and Marc get lost in a scary part of Queens, after Wilhelmina upsets their taxi driver. The Suarez family home in Jackson Heights is a real house in Queens.

EXTRA

INTERVIEWS

America Ferrera is Betty Suarez. America has great teeth and she doesn't wear glasses!

America Ferrera

Why did you take the part?

America: Betty is really clever. She cares about people and she loves almost everyone. She brings out the good in people. I thought, 'Wow! What a wonderful girl!'

Do you enjoy working on the show?

America: Everyone is brilliant on the show, and we all love each other. It feels like my family. We love our wonderful little world of Ugly Betty.

Do people stop you in the street all the time?

America: I spend a lot of time at work. I don't spend much time in the real world. The first time I had a break, I went to New York. People stopped me in the street every three metres: 'You're Betty! You're Betty!' they said.

with the Stars

Tony Plana

Ignacio is always cooking!

Tony: Ignacio's life is about the family. When he cooks for the family, he is taking care of them.

What's the show really about, do you think?

Tony: It's about important things. The Meade family has problems because they are rich. The Suarez family has problems because they are poor. Hilda didn't go to college, and she can't find a job. Betty went to college, and she gets a great job.

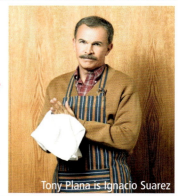
Tony Plana is Ignacio Suarez

Eric Mabius

Why do Daniel and Betty get on so well?

Eric: They come from very different worlds but they are both trying to find their way. Often they have the same problems in the same episode. They help each other and they do better together.

Describe Daniel!

Eric: I've never played a man like Daniel before. He's kind and he tries to be good. But often, he's just bad.

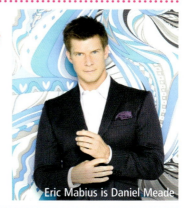
Eric Mabius is Daniel Meade

Vanessa Williams

How did you get the part?

Vanessa: I didn't know about the show until the day before filming. They rang me and said, 'We want you for Wilhelmina.'

Do you get on well with the other actors?

Vanessa: We really work together as a team. We're all different ages and backgrounds, and that's good.

Vanessa Williams is Wilhelmina Slater

EXTRA

INTERIORS: How to

The Suarez home is a real family home. There isn't much money, but there's a lot of life.

- Start your Suarez makeover with colours. Use different colours for the walls, sofa and rugs. The colours don't have to look good together.
- Put things everywhere – on the walls, on side tables, on the TV.
- Show your family photographs.
- Collect interesting pieces on holiday. They always look good when you get home.
- Can you have wallpaper with patterns next to curtains with flowers? Yes, you can!
- Forget cool! Go for warm.

What do these words mean? You can use a dictionary.
interior   rug   pattern   curtains

get the Suarez look

Show how you feel: These pieces from Mexico are about Home, Family and Fun.

INTERIORS.

Mode is a high fashion magazine. The *Mode* offices are high fashion offices. Here's how to get the look:

- Use white as your main colour and white as your second colour.
- Choose a shape and use it everywhere – for windows, lights, tables, everything. We chose circles.
- Find a good cleaner.
- Never drink coffee in the office.
- Find one or two pieces of colour. Wilhelmina has an orange telephone in her white room.

The creative director's office is the most stylish room in the building. Wilhelmina always puts herself first. She doesn't have comfortable sofas for her guests. She has a beautiful white sofa for herself.

**What do these words mean?
You can use a dictionary.**
shape   circle   stylish

get the *Mode* look

These cool, white pieces don't ask 'What are you like?' They ask 'What do you look like?'

EXTRA

FASHION: Cool or

▲ DANIEL MEADE, editor of *Mode*. This look says: 'I buy very expensive clothes, but I think about more important things than fashion.'

▼ BETTY SUAREZ, assistant to the editor.
This is not a good look. Do not copy it.

KEY:
▲ Cool!
▼ Not cool!

JUSTIN SUAREZ

▲ WILHELMINA SLATER, creative director of *Mode*. Clean lines and a beautiful style. You will never see this woman in jeans (except once in Series 1!).

50

▲ MARC ST JAMES, assistant to the creative director.
Brilliant! A cool grey business suit, with a lavender shirt. This really works.

▼ BETTY SUAREZ, again.
Oh, Betty! This is not a slimming look! Light blue does not work with red ... or any other colour.

▲ ALEXIS MEADE, editor of *Mode*.
Black, expensive, slimming, wonderful.

▲ AMANDA TANEN, receptionist at *Mode*.
Cool grey with a line of hot red. Amanda looks beautiful.

HOW TO ... be a good assistant to the editor
BY BETTY SUAREZ

1. When you answer the phone, say: 'Daniel Meade's office. This is Betty.' Don't say: 'I'm just finishing my bagel.'

2. Be careful of other office assistants when they are nice to you.
Amanda says: 'Betty, you look great today! I love your look!'
You don't say: 'Thank you, Amanda.'
You say: 'Amanda, what do you want?'

3. Always have some money with you. OK, so your boss is a millionaire ... you live in Queens ... your pay is a joke ... but *you'll* have to pay the two dollars for his Starbucks coffee.

4. Never wear shorts to the office. You will be the office joke. Marc will have a picture of you in shorts as his screensaver.

5. Not very thin? Then don't go to Christina's Free Clothes Day. Everything will be the smallest size and people will say things like this:
Wilhelmina: "Perhaps there are some socks in your size, Betty."

What do these words mean? You can use a dictionary.
advice   screensaver   carb (carbohydrates)   ice cream

Marc and Amanda

A good boss is a happy boss!
BY MARC ST JAMES

DOs
- Bring the right food on the right day. Tuesday is carb day.
- Tell your boss that she looks beautiful at least five times every day.
- Fashion houses will send you clothes for your boss. If something says size four inside, change it to size two.

DON'Ts
- Don't wear the same clothes as your boss.
- Don't let her see any ugly photos of herself.
- Don't have a noisy office chair. She won't like it.

He doesn't love you? Try these ideas!
BY AMANDA TANEN

Do you love someone but he doesn't love you? I know how you feel. I'm in love with Daniel. Try these ideas. They don't work for me, but maybe they will work for you. Good luck!

1. Tell him that you don't care about him.
2. Wear the same clothes as his girlfriend.
3. Tell him you are very busy. You go to a different party every night.
4. Always look fantastic!

If none of that works, sit on the sofa, eat a litre of ice cream and watch a sad DVD.

EPISODES 1–7

Before you read

You can use your dictionary.

1 Look at the 'New Words' at the back of the book. These people work on *Mode*. Who does what?

**accountant   assistant to the editor   creative director
editor   model   receptionist**

  a) Who appears in the pictures in *Mode*?

  b) Who is the boss of the magazine?

  c) Who plans the cover picture and the stories inside?

  d) Who controls the money?

  e) Who answers the phone and helps visitors to the magazine?

  f) Who answers the phone and keeps a diary for the editor?

2 Choose the correct word in *italics*.

  a) People sometimes take *pills/hearts* when they are not well.

  b) The opposite of beautiful is *fake/ugly*.

  c) If you *control/fire* someone, they lose their job.

  d) People get married *at a wedding/in a prison*.

3 Look at 'People and Places' on pages 4–5.

  a) Which is more fashionable – Manhattan or Queens?

  b) Who knows more about fashion – Betty or Amanda?

  c) Meade Publications owns *Mode* magazine. Who owns Meade – Bradford or Daniel?

  d) Who died in a sports accident – Rosa Suarez or Alex Meade?

  e) Who sells slimming pills – Wilhelmina or Hilda?

After you read

4 Match the two parts of these sentences.

  a) Daniel is very unkind to Betty   **i)** in the magazine.

  b) Everyone at *Mode* laughs   **ii)** in the United States.

  c) Natalie is pleased when her real photos appear   **iii)** on her first day.

  d) The expensive Gucci bag pays   **iv)** of another Meade magazine.

  e) Ignacio isn't allowed to work   **v)** at Betty's Queens makeover.

  f) Daniel falls in love with the editor   **vi)** for Ignacio's heart pills.

5 What do you think?
  a) Which is more important at a fashion magazine – what you look like or how you do your job?
  b) Would you like Betty's job at *Mode*? Why/Why not?

EPISODES 8–14

Before you read
6 What will happen next?
  a) Sofia will fall in love with Daniel and they will have a wedding.
  b) Sofia will offer Betty a good job on her magazine.
  c) Wilhelmina will get Daniel's job.

After you read
7 Correct these sentences.
  a) Betty is upset because Daniel doesn't like her hotel story.
  b) Sofia's boyfriend is dark, ugly and boring.
  c) Wilhelmina takes control of the Baby Chutney photo shoot.
  d) Betty enjoys Walter's Christmas party.
  e) Sofia is really in love with Daniel.
  f) Daniel goes to Rio for two weeks.
  g) Betty offers Hilda a job at Fashion Week.

8 What are the names?
  a) Who prefers Atlantic City to an expensive Manhattan hotel?
  b) Who is Justin's father?
  c) Who has heard bad stories about Hilda's cheap lawyer?
  d) Who was editor of *Mode* before Daniel?
  e) Who kisses a supermodel at the *Mode* Christmas party?
  f) Who takes a letter about Bradford Meade to the police for Wilhelmina?
  g) Who does everyone love at Fashion Week?
  h) Who suddenly appears at the *Mode* party?
  i) Who do the police take to prison?

9 What do you think?
  Sofia plays a trick on Daniel. She isn't really in love with him, but she

wants a story about him for her magazine. Is it OK to trick someone for a magazine story? Why/why not?

EPISODES 15–23

Before you read
10 What will happen next?
   a) Bradford will stay in prison because he killed Fey.
   b) Alexis and Wilhelmina will take control of *Mode*.
   c) Daniel will fight Alexis and keep his job as editor.

After you read
11 Answer these questions.
   a) Did Bradford Meade kill Fey Summers?
   b) Do Betty and Charlie go to the fashion party?
   c) Does Alexis want to help Bradford?
   d) Does Daniel plan to fight Alexis for *Mode*?
   e) Does Betty feel she has good friends at *Mode*?
   f) Santos asks Hilda to marry him. Does she say yes or no?
   g) Is Rodrigo really in love with Alexis?
   h) What secret does Betty learn about her family in Mexico?

12 Put these sentences in the right order.
   a) Betty and Henry say goodbye.
   b) Betty and Walter break up.
   c) Betty invites Henry to Queens for supper.
   d) Charlie arrives and tells Betty, 'I am going to have Henry's baby.'
   e) Charlie decides to stay in New York.
   f) Henry can't go to the show because his old girlfriend is here.
   g) Henry fights for Betty at Office Assistants' Day.
   h) Henry invites Betty to a show and she says yes.
   i) Henry tells Betty he has finished with Charlie.

13 What do you think?
   Before she died, Betty's mother said to Betty, 'The most important thing in life is to find someone who loves you.' Do you agree?